Catching Cam's Balloon

John Parker
Illustrated by Nick Buttfield

Contents

ETA Cuisenaire

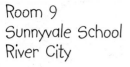

Room 9
Sunnyvale School
River City

Tuesday

Dear Mr. Costa,
I'm sorry I was late for school yesterday.
I'm sorry that my excuse didn't make sense.

You told me to write you a letter.
You said that would make it easier to understand.
You said it would be good writing practice, too.

So here's my letter.
It's so long, I've added chapters.

CHAPTER 1

To the Rescue

That morning, I had plenty of time to catch the school bus.
I was saying goodbye to my little brother Cam.

Cam was holding a big, orange balloon.
The balloon was left over from his birthday party.
Cam took that balloon everywhere. He loved it!

Cam was waving goodbye to me. But he waved so
hard, he let go of the balloon string.
It was a windy day, Mr. Costa.
The wind blew Cam's balloon away.
Cam started crying.
He wanted his balloon back.

WAAH!

I told Cam it would be all right.

Don't worry. I'll get your balloon back.
I'll get it before the bus comes.

5

CHAPTER 2

Oops!

It didn't happen like that, Mr. Costa.
I didn't get the balloon back before the bus came.

That balloon was so fast!
I ran so hard that my legs almost flew off.
It was no use.
I still couldn't catch that balloon.

The wind blew the balloon around a corner.
I ran around the corner as fast as I could.
I know I should have slowed down.
I ran straight into a man.

CRUNCH!

The man fell down on the sidewalk.
Everything spilled out of his bag.
Beans and carrots and potatoes and onions
rolled everywhere.
It was vegetable soup, Mr. Costa!
The man yelled.

Help! Police!

He thought I wanted to steal his vegetables!

I had to keep going.

I couldn't stop to help the man, Mr. Costa.
I had to catch that balloon.
Cam would cry for a week if I didn't come home
with the balloon.
Our neighbors would move out
because of his screaming!

The wind blew the balloon up into the air.
It landed on top of Mr. Vango's Pet Shop.
I climbed on the fence and reached out for the balloon.

I had to stretch...

and stretch...

...and stretch.

CHAPTER 3

Things Get Worse

It didn't happen like that, Mr. Costa.
I didn't climb down. I fell down instead.
All the pets in Mr. Vango's shop wanted to tell
the whole world about me.

It was so embarrassing.
I had to explain everything to Mr. Vango.
Then I had to give Cam his balloon.
Then I had to catch the bus to school.

It didn't happen like that, Mr. Costa.
I heard a police whistle.
I guessed that the man had told the police about me.
A police officer was after me!

I was so surprised that I let go of the string.
The wind blew the balloon away again.

I couldn't stop to explain to the police officer.
The balloon would have disappeared if I'd stopped.
So I kept running.

I looked back. Mr. Vango had come out of his shop
to see what all the fuss was about.
The police officer ran into him.
Then they both fell over.

That helped me get away from them.
The balloon blew into Mrs. Lu's Fruit Shop.
I ran after it.

I couldn't see the balloon at first.
Then I saw it. It was at the back of the shop.
It was trying to hide on a big pile of orange pumpkins!

CHAPTER 4

Tricky!

Reaching the balloon was going to be tricky.
The pile of pumpkins was big!
I should have asked Mrs. Lu for a ladder.

But I didn't ask for a ladder.

Instead, I stood on my toes.
Then I reached up carefully toward the balloon.
I must have looked like a crazy ballet dancer.

I had almost reached it when the police officer burst in.

I didn't hold it.
I lost my balance and crashed into the pumpkins.

Pumpkins rolled everywhere.
It was a pumpkin avalanche!
The police officer tried to get out of the way,
but the pumpkins tripped him.

Now I was worried.
I thought he'd arrest me and send me to jail.
So I explained everything to him – fast!

Do you know what, Mr. Costa?
The police officer laughed until he was red in the face.
He said it was the funniest story he'd ever heard.
He said he'd help me look for the balloon, too.

CHAPTER 5

The End

We soon found the balloon in Mrs. Lu's shop.
The balloon was sitting on the lettuce.
I think it wanted to give itself up.

I told the police officer I wouldn't run too fast
around corners again.
Then I went home to give the balloon to Cam.

But it wasn't worth it, Mr. Costa.

Cam said he didn't want the balloon anymore.

He gave it a kick.

The balloon burst.

Cam   me

And that's why I was late for school, Mr. Costa.

Yours truly,

Max